Simplified Estate Accounting

A Guide for Executors,
Trustees, and Attorneys

Donna S.M. Neff, JD, TEP

eNeff Enterprises

www.eNeffEnterprises.com

Simplified Estate Accounting, by Donna S.M. Neff

First Edition, July 2011

Copyright © 2002-2011 Donna S. M. Neff

Author Services by Pedernales Publishing, LLC.
www.pedernalespublishing.com

Published by eNeff Enterprises, Ottawa, Ontario, Canada

No part of this book may be reproduced in any form or by any electronic or mechanical means including information storage and retrieval systems, without permission in writing from the author. The only exception is by a reviewer, who may quote short excerpts in a review. For more information contact the author by email at:

info@eneffenterprises.com
www.eneffenterprises.com

Legal Disclaimer

The information contained in this guide is intended solely to provide general guidance on matters of interest for the personal use of the reader, who accepts full responsibility for its use. The information is provided with the understanding that the author and publisher are not retained and are not rendering legal, accounting, tax, or other professional advice or services. As such, this guide should not be used as a substitute for consultation.

While the author and publisher have made every attempt to ensure the information contained in this guide is accurate, Donna S.M. Neff and eNeff Enterprises are not responsible for any errors or omissions, or for the results obtained from the use of this information. All information in this guide is provided "as is," with no guarantee of completeness, accuracy, timeliness or of the results obtained from the use of this information, and without warranty of any kind, express or implied. Nothing herein shall to any extent substitute for the independent investigation and the sound judgment of the reader. Laws and regulations are continually changing and can be interpreted only in light of particular factual situations.

Excel™ is a registered trademark of Microsoft Corporation

ISBN: 978-0-9869218-0-3

Printed in the United States of America

Contents

1. Introduction — 1
Is This Guide for You? — 1
    Executors and Trustees — 2
    Attorneys for Property — 3
    Compensation — 4
What This Guide is Not — 4
Glossary & the Meaning of 'Attorney' — 5
When Does an Executor, Trustee, or Attorney Have Authority — 5
Key Players — 6
What is a Passing of Accounts? — 8
The Purpose of Estate Accounting — 9
Young Beneficiaries or Minors — 10
Incapable Beneficiaries or Incapable Grantors — 11
Sample Spreadsheets — 12

2. The Pieces of the Puzzle — 15
Introduction — 15
Handling the Money — 15
What It Means to 'Realize' an Asset — 16
Sections of an Accounting Report — 17
    Title Page — 17
    Table of Contents — 18
    Summary & Reconciliation — 18
    Statement of Assets — 19
    Receipts — 22
    Disbursements — 23
    Investment Account — 24
    Statement of Assets at the End of the Period — 25
    Statement of Compensation — 25

Additional Sections That May be Needed If It is Not the Final Accounting Period	25
Investments at the End of the Period	26
Statement of Unrealized Assets at the End of the Period	26
Statement of Outstanding Liabilities	26
Assets Held in a Foreign Currency	26
What to Look for if the 'Summary & Reconciliation' Worksheet Cannot Be Reconciled	27
Dealing with Mutual Funds	28
Investrack	28
3. Calculating Compensation	**31**
When Compensation Can Be Paid	31
Compensation for an Executor or a Trustee	32
Compensation for an Attorney	33
Factors Considered by a Judge When Reviewing Compensation	33
Compensation Calculations in the Spreadsheets	35
Pre-paid Funeral Expenses, Out of Pocket Expenses	36
Compensation on Tax Refunds	36
Conclusion	36
Glossary	37
Acknowledgements	41
About the Author	43

1. Introduction

Is This Guide for You?

If you are considering, or are already, acting as an executor or trustee of a simple estate or trust or if you are acting or have been named as an attorney for property for someone who is of modest means, this guide is for you. If so, consider reading through this short guide (just three chapters in length plus the glossary) before focusing on any particular section. When you are done, you should have a general understanding of the accounting and record-keeping which come with the job you've taken on, or are about to take on.

After an initial read-through, go back to specific sections as needed so that you can set up and maintain organized, detailed records. Why is record-keeping so important? As an executor, trustee, or attorney, you will eventually be answerable to someone. You will need to be able to explain what you have done with the assets under your care and control. In addition, if you want to be paid for the work that you do, detailed accounting records are essential to determining how much you can be paid.

Although most of us tend to think of an 'estate' as being what a deceased person owned at the date of death, the term 'estate' also means the whole of a person's possessions whether that person is living or deceased. In reading this guide, think of the broader meaning of 'estate' especially where the context suggests that it isn't just the assets of a deceased that are under discussion.

SIMPLIFIED ESTATE ACCOUNTING

Estate accounts are in a format that is not used by anyone in a commercial, investment, or bookkeeping role. They are antique and specialized. They take their form because of a historical need to keep track of the income and capital separately, usually because there were different beneficiaries for income and for capital.

Although this guide is intended primarily for use in Ontario estates, it may be helpful if you are handling affairs in another jurisdiction. It may also be helpful if you are an executor, trustee, attorney for property, or guardian of property and do not intend to prepare the estate accounts personally but would like a better understanding of what is involved.

In this chapter, we set the stage by explaining essential terms and concepts. The second chapter gets into the nitty-gritty of estate accounting, what information is tracked, and how it is arranged in the estate accounts. In the final chapter, we explain how to get paid for what you do. Even if you think you do not want to be paid, you may re-consider after you have been 'on the job' for a while. Being an executor, trustee, or attorney for property is not a 'walk in the park' even if the assets that you are managing are modest.

Before we go any further, let's make sure we have a clear understanding of what defines an executor, a trustee, and an attorney for property.

Executors and Trustees

The assets of an estate may be managed by an executor who is named in a will or who is appointed by court order if there is no will. The assets of a trust are managed by a trustee who may have been named in a will, appointed by court order, or named in a trust document. In terms of managing assets, the duties and responsibilities of a trustee are similar to those of an executor.

Attorneys for Property

The financial affairs of a living person may be managed by an attorney for property who is named in a Power of Attorney document signed by a 'grantor'. The terms of the Power of Attorney document might specify that the attorney for property can only act while the grantor is mentally incapable.

If the Power of Attorney document does not include a condition that the grantor must be mentally incapable, the attorney can act while the grantor is mentally capable or incapable. As a result, the attorney can act even if the grantor is mentally fine but unable to manage his or her affairs for any number of reasons. The grantor might be travelling for an extended period, suffering from grief, depression, or declining memory, or looking after an ill spouse or relative.

Alternatively, the financial affairs of a living person may be managed by a guardian of property appointed by court order or as a result of an application to replace the Public Guardian and Trustee as statutory guardian. The roles of an attorney for property and a guardian of property are similar but the basis of their authority is different. This guide is not intended for use by guardians of property. However, reading this guide can provide an understanding of the detailed accounting that will eventually be required of a guardian of property.

Compensation

This guide may also be helpful for determining the amount of compensation (payment for work done) that an executor, a trustee, or an attorney might reasonably charge. *Chapter 3, Calculating Compensation*, provides a detailed discussion of how to calculate compensation and when it may be paid.

What This Guide is Not

This publication is not intended as a comprehensive guide for anyone who may be required to, or who plans to, voluntarily have his or her accounts approved by a court (see *What is a Passing of Accounts?*, later in chapter). A guardian of property, in particular, is generally required to pass his or her accounts on a regular basis as stated in the court order by which he or she was appointed. For this reason, a guardian of property is rarely mentioned in this guide even though the reporting requirements may, in fact, be applicable to a guardian of property.

This guide does not provide investment or financial planning advice for an executor, trustee, or attorney. Such advice should be obtained from a financial planning professional who is familiar with the standards that an executor, trustee, or attorney must meet and who can assist in developing a financial plan. At an initial meeting with the financial planning professional, the executor, trustee, or attorney will want to provide the professional with a list of the assets being managed, whether there is a need for money on an on-going basis, and how long the investments are likely to be managed.

In the case of a trustee or attorney, the health and life expectancy of the trust beneficiary or grantor will also be a factor to be considered when developing a financial plan. With this information, the financial planning professional will be better able to recommend an investment strategy that ensures the funds will be managed in the best possible manner.

Glossary & the Meaning of 'Attorney'

At the back of this guide is a *Glossary*. It lists terms which might be unfamiliar or which may have a different meaning than expected. For example, the word 'attorney' is generally used in Ontario to mean a substitute decision-maker while in the USA it is used to mean a lawyer. It is listed in the *Glossary* to ensure that its meaning in Canada (and in this guide) is clear.

In this guide, 'attorney' means a substitute decision-maker who has been named to take care of a person's financial affairs (attorney for property). 'Attorney' may also mean a person named in a Power of Attorney for Personal Care to make a medical treatment or other personal care decision for a person who is unable to do so.

To add to the confusion, in Ontario a lawyer can be named to act as an attorney; however, the attorney or substitute decision-maker need not be a lawyer.

When Does an Executor, Trustee, or Attorney Have Authority

There is often confusion about when the executor's, trustee's, or attorney's authority begins and ends. An executor takes care of someone's estate after the person has died. Until the person's death, the executor has no authority. Executrix is the feminine form of executor. Throughout this guide, we use the term 'executor' to refer to the person in that role whether male or female.

A trustee, on the other hand, may have authority before or after death depending upon how, why, and when the trust was established. If the trust was established as a result of a death, it is referred to as a 'testamentary trust'. A trust established by someone during his or her lifetime is referred to as an 'inter-vivos trust'. There are certain tax advantages for a testamentary trust (such as a potentially lower tax rate) which are not available for an inter-vivos trust. However, to preserve those tax advantages, compliance with certain tax rules is required.

An attorney acts for someone while that person is alive. The attorney's authority ends on the death of that person. In other words, the validity of the Power of Attorney document dies with the person who signed it, that is, the grantor.

Key Players

If you are an executor or a trustee, the key players can include:

- **beneficiaries** – the individuals, charities or other entities named in the will of the deceased or, if there is no will, the beneficiaries listed in the *Succession Law Reform Act* (typically the spouse and/or children, then parents, siblings, and other relatives according to the list set out in the Act) or the person or persons who are to benefit from a trust,
- **creditors** – a person, company, or other entity who is owed money by the deceased or the trust,

INTRODUCTION

- **minor beneficiary** – anyone under the age of 18 who is receiving a portion or all of an estate or trust,

- **incapable beneficiary** – anyone who is receiving a portion or all of an estate or income or capital from a trust and who is mentally incapable as defined by the *Substitute Decisions Act,*

- **estate trustee** – in Ontario, another name for an executor. An executor named in a will is referred to as an *Estate Trustee with a Will*. A person carrying out the duties of an executor and who is not named in a will (because there is no will) but has been appointed by court order is referred to as an *Estate Trustee without a Will,*

- **trustee** – a person appointed by a will, by a trust agreement, or by court order to administer a trust for a trust beneficiary,

- **Public Guardian and Trustee (PGT)** – an Ontario government agency that must be provided with the accounts of an executor or trustee if a beneficiary who is 18 or older is mentally incapable when the executor or trustee presents the accounts to the court for approval,

- **Office of the Children's Lawyer (OCL)** – an Ontario government agency which must be provided with the estate or trust accounts if a beneficiary is under the age of 18 when an executor or trustee presents his or her accounts to the court for approval.

If you are acting as an attorney for property, key players can include:

- **grantor** – the person who has signed a document called a Power of Attorney for Property in which she or he names an attorney and 'grants' the attorney the authority to look after her or his financial affairs. If it is a <u>Continuing</u> Power of Attorney for Property, the attorney for property can <u>continue</u> to take care of the grantor's financial affairs even if the grantor is declared mentally incapable,

- **interested parties** – the family and close relatives of the grantor or a beneficiary (relative or not) who is named in the grantor's will, or someone who has a financial interest in the affairs of the grantor such as a creditor or a potential beneficiary of the grantor's estate where there is no will,

- **Public Guardian and Trustee (PGT)** – an Ontario government agency that must be provided with the accounts of an attorney for property if the grantor is mentally incapable when the attorney presents the accounts to the court for approval.

What is a Passing of Accounts?

A passing of accounts is a formal court process to have the accounting records of an executor, a trustee, or an attorney for property approved by the court. A passing of accounts is required if there are any objections to the accounting records, if a beneficiary or other affected person either will not or cannot approve the accounts, or if a passing is required by court order.

For example, if one of the beneficiaries of an estate or a trust is mentally incapable or is under the age of 18 (a 'minor'), the executor or trustee will be required to pass his or her accounts.

An attorney for property could be required to pass her or his accounts if someone asks the court for an order requiring a passing. A dependant, the PGT, a creditor, or the grantor himself/herself, if capable, can apply to the court for an order requiring an attorney to pass his or her accounts.

INTRODUCTION

An executor, trustee, or attorney for property may voluntarily submit his or her accounts to a judge for approval. This might be done to have the court 'bless' the executor's, trustee's, or attorney's accounts in order for the executor, trustee, or attorney to be exonerated (relieved of any legal liability) for a defined period of administration. The court also determines and approves the amount of compensation which is due to the executor, trustee, or attorney for property.

Once the accounts are approved or 'passed' and if there is no appeal, the executor, trustee, or attorney is released from further liability for those transactions that were reported in the accounting and the amount of compensation is approved. If a passing of accounts for an estate is necessary, it is important that it be completed before the final distribution.

If a passing of accounts is necessary or desirable, the accounting records should be produced in a more formal court format. In addition, certain legal documents must be prepared, including a Notice of Application, a sworn affidavit, and other documents required by the court. These must be submitted along with the estate accounting report and court filing fees. Additional procedural requirements such as 'service' of documents on certain parties must also be completed within specific time limits.

The Purpose of Estate Accounting

The two main reasons for preparing an accounting report are:

1. To provide a detailed report of how the executor, trustee, or attorney for property has handled the assets

and liabilities under his or her care and control so that beneficiaries, the grantor, the PGT, and others who have a right to know can review and approve (or not) what has been done, and,

2. To calculate the amount of compensation if taken.

The amount of compensation is subject to approval by a judge. If there are no objections to the accounting and if none of the beneficiaries are mentally incapable or under the age of 18, the accounts may be passed 'on consent' without a court appearance.

Estate accounting must be accurate to the penny – no rounding or approximating is allowed. The estate accounting report must show everything in perfect balance (more on how to do this in *Chapter 2, The Pieces of the Puzzle*). It must be possible to trace where every asset came from, what has happened to it while under the care and control of the executor, trustee, or attorney, and where it ended up.

Throughout this guide, the importance of careful, detailed record-keeping is emphasized and with good reason. As an executor, trustee, or attorney, you will want to show that you have carried out your duties and responsibilities with the utmost of care and planning. You need to be prepared to answer questions asked by those who have a right to know what you have done with the assets such as estate or trust beneficiaries, the grantor, the PGT, the OCL, or a judge.

Young Beneficiaries or Minors

Special considerations arise when there are minor or unborn beneficiaries. A minor is a person under the age of 18. If a minor is entitled to a share of an estate or a trust, the Office of the Children's Lawyer (OCL) must be notified. The OCL must also be notified if there is an unborn beneficiary of an estate or trust. Many parents are surprised to learn that they do not have the right to approve the accounts of an executor or trustee on behalf of their minor or unborn children.

Under the *Estates Act* if there is a minor or unborn beneficiary, the OCL must be provided with the estate or trust accounts when an executor or trustee presents his or her accounts to the court for approval.

Only a court can approve the accounts of an executor or an attorney on behalf of a minor or the unborn.

The OCL does not have authority to administer estates or trusts and does not act as guardian of property for a minor.

Incapable Beneficiaries or Incapable Grantors

A person who is 18 or older but who "is not able to understand information that is relevant to making a decision in the management of his or her property, or is not able to appreciate the reasonably foreseeable consequences of a decision or lack of decision" is mentally incapable under Ontario law (see the *Substitute Decisions Act*).

A mentally incapable beneficiary of an estate or trust cannot approve the accounts of an executor or trustee. When an executor or trustee presents his or her accounts to the court for approval, the PGT must be provided with the estate or trust accounts if any beneficiary is mentally incapable.

Similarly, a mentally incapable grantor cannot approve the accounts of an attorney for property. When an attorney for property presents his or her accounts to the court for approval, the PGT must be provided with the accounts.

Only a court can approve the accounts of an executor, trustee, or attorney on behalf of a mentally incapable person.

Sample Spreadsheets

Readers of this guide have access to sample Excel™ spreadsheets which may be downloaded from www.eneffenterprises.com/spreadsheet.htm. The spreadsheets are 'read-only' which means that the original files on our website cannot be accidentally modified.

After opening the spreadsheet file that you need, save it on your computer under a new name. It is assumed that you have a basic understanding of Excel and how it works. You can make as many backups or copies of the spreadsheets as you want. There are three sets of spreadsheets – one for use by each of the following:

1. an executor,
2. an attorney for property,
3. a trustee of a trust.

The formula for calculating compensation for an executor and for a trustee is not the same as for an attorney for property. For this reason, it is important that you use the correct set of spreadsheets. See *Chapter 3, Calculating Compensation*.

INTRODUCTION

This guide and the associated spreadsheets are not intended for tracking an estate or the property of a person if the assets and related transactions are numerous or complex nor is it intended for an estate or an on-going trust with substantial assets. However, it may be adequate for a simple trust such as one set up for the recipient of a disability pension who needs to shelter an inheritance of less than $100,000.00.

If the financial transactions to be tracked do not fall within the scope of this guide or if it is possible a passing of accounts will be necessary or desirable (see *What is a Passing of Accounts?* earlier in this chapter), we recommend seeking the assistance of a professional who is familiar with the preparation of estate accounting in court format. However, this guide may be helpful to gain a basic understanding of this specialized type of accounting and the kind of information that is needed by the person who is preparing the accounts.

2. The Pieces of the Puzzle

Introduction

This chapter provides some basic guidelines about how to handle the funds, explains what is meant by 'realizing' an asset, and describes the major sections found in an estate accounting report and what each section typically contains. As you read through this chapter, it will be helpful to have a printout of the sample spreadsheets handy or have the sample spreadsheets open on your computer.

In most sections of an estate accounting report, entries are numbered consecutively to simplify cross-referencing from one section to another. With certain exceptions, entries within a section are arranged in chronological order by transaction date.

Handling the Money

It goes without saying that estate or trust funds or the funds of a grantor must never be mixed with the personal funds of the executor, trustee, or attorney.

When acting as an executor, simplify the accounting by using one bank account for all deposits and for paying bills. Do not use cash to pay bills or to reimburse yourself for expenses. If cash is found in the deceased's home, deposit it into the bank account and then write cheques to pay bills or to reimburse yourself.

Similarly, if you are acting as an attorney for property, simplify things as much as possible by limiting the number of bank accounts and investment accounts that you must track. However, if the grantor had more than one or two bank accounts or multiple investment accounts, before making significant changes review the financial and tax impact of such changes with a professional advisor.

When acting as trustee on behalf of a trust beneficiary, the beneficiary's own assets should never be mixed in with trust assets. In fact, nothing must ever be deposited into the trust bank account or the trust investment account unless it is income or dividends earned by the trust or the proceeds received from the sale of a trust asset. If money or assets which were not initially trust assets are added to a trust, the trust's tax status could be affected (and not in a good way). Once money is paid out of the trust, it should usually not be deposited back into the trust (unless money is being moved around for investment purposes and the owner of the investment is always the trust).

What It Means to 'Realize' an Asset

It is important to understand what is meant by 'realizing an asset'. Generally, an asset is 'realized' when it is turned into cash or other readily-negotiable form while under the control of the executor, trustee, or attorney. Several examples will help illustrate what is meant by 'realizing an asset'.

When a cottage that is part of an estate is sold and the sale proceeds are invested, the cottage asset is realized as of the date that it is sold.

A Canada Savings Bond (CSB) reaches maturity and is cashed out and the proceeds are deposited to the estate account (or trust account or grantor's account). The amount received including interest is realized as of the date that the CSB is cashed out.

An insurance company issues a cheque payable to the estate upon the death of the life insured. The policy is realized as of the date that the cheque is received.

Sections of an Accounting Report

Title Page

For the accounts of an executor, the title page includes:

- name of the deceased,
- date of death,
- role and name of the person reporting. The role will usually be either:
    - Estate Trustee with a Will or
    - Estate Trustee without a Will, and
- period being reported (the start and end dates of the period covered by the report).

For the accounts of a trustee, the title page includes:

- name of the trust beneficiary,
- name of the trustee, and
- period being reported (the start and end dates of the period covered by the report).

For the accounts of an attorney for property, the title page includes:

- name of the grantor,
- role and name of the person reporting. The role will generally be 'attorney for property' unless acting under a guardianship order, and
- period being reported (the start and end dates of the period covered by the report).

Table of Contents

Although not mandatory, it is helpful to include a table of contents which lists the sections in the order in which they appear in the report.

Summary & Reconciliation

This section of the report is usually no more than one page. It lists totals for receipts (money and other items received), disbursements (money or other items paid out or 'disbursed'), and investments in the reporting period.

If you use the spreadsheets provided and if none of the formulas have been modified, the *Summary and Reconciliation* worksheet is automatically filled in with totals for each of:

- receipts,
- disbursements, and
- investments.

The balance (at the bottom) should always equal zero. If not, either the formulas have been inadvertently changed or something is out of balance elsewhere in the accounts. To help you figure out what might be causing the problem, see *What to Look for if the 'Summary & Reconciliation' Worksheet Cannot Be Reconciled* later in this chapter.

Statement of Assets

The statement of assets provides a detailed list of all assets owned at the start of the reporting period. If the reporting period is not the first period, this title might be modified to *Statement of Assets at the Beginning of the Period*. The start date is one of:

- if acting as an executor of an estate, the date of death,
- if acting as a trustee, the date of death of the person whose will included a trust, otherwise, the date specified in the trust document;
- if acting as an attorney for property, the date that the attorney took charge of the grantor's financial affairs,
- if an accounting has previously been submitted and approved, the start date of the next reporting period is the day following the end of the previous reporting period.

Assets include everything in which the deceased had any ownership rights at date of death, or what a trust owns such as distributions from an estate or what a grantor owned on the date when the attorney took over.

For a deceased person who had established a Registered Education Savings Plan (RESP) for a child, the RESP is an asset of the estate if the deceased was the sole subscriber and did not name a successor subscriber in his or her will. A discussion of how to deal with an RESP is not within the scope of this guide.

SIMPLIFIED ESTATE ACCOUNTING

The kinds of assets that might be included in an estate accounting report are many and varied. The list below is not exhaustive but includes many of the most common kinds of assets that there might be:

- bank accounts,
- guaranteed investment certificates (or GIC's, also known by several other names depending upon the financial institution such as a certificate of deposit),
- investment accounts,
- stocks,
- mutual funds,
- registered education savings plan (RESP) under certain circumstances as mentioned above,
- registered retirement savings account (RRSP),
- locked-in retirement account (LIRA),
- tax free savings account (TFSA),
- registered retirement income fund (RRIF),
- registered disability savings plan (RDSP),
- life insurance,
- death benefits if payable to the estate,
- bonds such as corporate bonds, Canada Savings Bonds (CSB's), or other government bonds,
- house, cottage, or other real property,
- vehicles, boats, RV's,
- household goods and personal effects such as artwork, jewellery, tools,

- pre-paid funeral, and
- share of an estate (an inheritance that has not yet been received).

Note that an estate will only be a beneficiary of an RRSP, RRIF, life insurance, or similar asset if the estate is the named beneficiary, or if no one has been named as a beneficiary, or if the named beneficiary is not alive at the death of the owner and no contingent or alternate beneficiary has been named.

If the asset is a bank account, include the name and address of the bank, the account number, type of account, and the account balance on the start date.

If the asset is a stock or mutual fund, list the name of the stock or mutual fund, share certificate number, the type and number of shares or units, and when they were acquired or bought.

Some assets can be difficult to value but every asset must be included and a reasonable attempt made to determine a value for each asset. Appraisals of some items may be desirable or even necessary where the value as of the date of death is needed for determining capital gains or losses for tax reporting purposes. If all the assets of an estate are being distributed to one beneficiary and if there is no need for an appraisal to satisfy income tax reporting or other requirements, it may not be necessary to have an appraisal done for some assets. However, note that in Ontario executors will soon be required to have proof of the value of all estate assets so that government officials can be assured that the amount of probate fees were properly calculated.

SIMPLIFIED ESTATE ACCOUNTING

Although RRSPs, LIRAs, RRIFs, and similar assets may be paid directly to a named beneficiary, the estate is generally liable for any income tax owing with respect to all such assets. However, if the beneficiary is a spouse, income tax might be deferred.

For some items, the value at the time of the accounting may be significantly different than the value on the start date. For example, the value of stocks can differ dramatically from the beginning to the end of the period which is being reported. However, when listing stocks in the *Statement of Assets* the value to be listed is the fair market value as of the start date of the period being reported. If the start date falls on a weekend or holiday, use the value as of the business day immediately before the start date.

In the *Statement of Assets* include as much detail as possible to clearly identify the asset. It is always better to include too much detail than not enough.

Receipts

A receipt is generally anything of value received by the estate, the trust, or the grantor. An asset is not usually listed as received until it is realized. An exception is a bank account which is usually realized as of the start date of the first reporting period.

In some accounting reports, receipts may need to be reported as either a *Capital Receipt* or a *Revenue Receipt*. This is necessary if a trust has a beneficiary who is to receive income from the trust while another beneficiary is to receive the capital of the trust when the trust ends. For many small estates or trusts, separating receipts into 'capital' and 'revenue' is not usually necessary. However, it is important to understand the difference in case you need to report them separately.

A Capital Receipt is an original asset as of the start date. Capital gains and certain tax refunds may also be capital receipts.

A Revenue Receipt is income received after the start date such as pensions, interest income, dividends, refunds, Canada Pension Plan (CPP) payments, Old Age Security (OAS) payments, superannuation, and any other income received. Note that an estate is entitled to keep CPP, OAS and similar income which is received in the month of death even if paid after the date of death.

Disbursements

A disbursement is money paid out of an estate including payments to beneficiaries, probate fees, legal fees, funeral expenses, and other expenses that result from the death of the individual. For a trust, disbursements include expenses relating to the operation of the trust and payments to trust beneficiaries. For a grantor, disbursements are typically living expenses, legal fees, income taxes and so on. In all cases, payment of compensation to the executor, trustee, or attorney (see next chapter) is also a disbursement.

Disbursements may need to be reported as either a *Capital Disbursement* or a *Revenue Disbursement*. This is necessary if the will or the terms of the trust indicate that a beneficiary is to receive income from the trust while a different beneficiary is to receive the capital of the trust.

Capital Disbursements of an estate include payments to beneficiaries, probate fees, legal fees, funeral expenses, and other expenses that result from the death of the individual. Capital losses are recorded as capital disbursements. For a trust, disbursements include payments to or for a trust beneficiary.

Revenue Disbursements are regular expenses of the estate or trust such as bank fees, investment fees, and so on.

Investment Account

An accounting report for a more complex estate or trust or for a wealthy grantor will include an *Investment Account* section to show transactions relating to investments made by the executor, trustee, or attorney. If investments include mutual funds, the monthly value of mutual fund holdings must be tracked. To assist with tracking this value, included in the spreadsheets is a worksheet called *Investrack* described in *Dealing with Mutual Funds* later in this chapter. The *Investrack* worksheets are not included in the final accounting report. They are used for tracking purposes only.

The *Investment Account* section includes all investments made by an executor, trustee, or attorney during the reporting period. There are separate debit and credit columns to show the in's and out's of investment monies. It does not include original assets which were not purchased by the executor, trustee, or attorney. When these are realized, they are reported in *Capital Receipts*.

For example, if the deceased owned a 5-year bond before his or her date of death, and the bond matured six months after the date of death, the realization of that bond is included in the list of *Capital Receipts*. However, if the funds from the realization of that bond are invested in another bond, the purchase of the second bond will be included in the *Investment Account* as a debit. When the second bond is cashed out, it is listed in the *Investment Account* as a credit.

THE PIECES OF THE PUZZLE

At the end of the *Investment Account* section, subtotals of all debits and all credits are shown. Below the subtotals, the balance invested is shown. This number should be the debits minus the credits. The balance invested must equal the total of *Investments at the End of the Period* (see below).

Purchases, gains, and reinvested dividends are entered as debits. Sales and losses are entered as credits. When all entries have been completed, the *Investment Account* balance for each investment being tracked must match the *Investrack* worksheet total for that investment (see *Dealing With Mutual Funds* later in this chapter).

Statement of Assets at the End of the Period

This includes all assets being held at the end of the reporting period.

Statement of Compensation

This shows detailed calculations as to how the total amount of compensation was determined. For a discussion as to what is included and how to take into account items which are 'non-compensable', see *Chapter 3, Calculating Compensation*.

Additional Sections That May be Needed If It is Not the Final Accounting Period

If assets will continue to be managed beyond the end of the reporting period and there will be further accounting reports in the future, include these sections as needed:

- Investments at the End of the Period,
- Statement of Unrealized Assets at the End of the Period, and
- Statement of Outstanding Liabilities.

Investments at the End of the Period

This section lists all investments that have not been realized at the end of the accounting period. In addition to the value on the date it was purchased, all details of each investment are listed. If the asset is a mutual fund investment, copy the *Investrack* worksheet so that you can track the value of each mutual fund investment (see *Dealing with Mutual Funds* later in this chapter).

Statement of Unrealized Assets at the End of the Period

This section provides a detailed list of all assets which were owned but not realized before the start of the period and were still not realized when the reporting period ended.

Statement of Outstanding Liabilities

This section lists all unpaid liabilities and can include both real (known but not yet paid) and contingent (estimated or expected but not yet certain) liabilities.

Assets Held in a Foreign Currency

If holding funds in any currency other than Canadian dollars, the foreign exchange gain or loss must be calculated each month.

THE PIECES OF THE PUZZLE

To determine the foreign exchange gain or loss, calculate the difference between the exchange rate at the beginning of the month and the exchange rate at the end of the month then multiply the difference by the amount of the funds being held throughout the month. The result is the gain or loss for the month.

If a transaction occurred during the month for any funds in a foreign currency, calculate the foreign exchange gain or loss for each transaction based on the difference in exchange rates between the rate on the date of the transaction and the rate at the end of the month.

What to Look for if the 'Summary & Reconciliation' Worksheet Cannot Be Reconciled

The balance on the *Summary & Reconciliation* worksheet should be zero. If it is not, check the following:

1. Have the account balances been entered on the summary page including any cash balance in investment accounts? Ensure any foreign currency accounts (and any additional transactions) have been converted to Canadian dollars.

2. Are all transactions within the date range of the accounting report and referenced correctly on the *Summary & Reconciliation* worksheet?

3. Has the foreign exchange gain or loss, if applicable, been properly calculated and entered in the correct section, e.g., a foreign exchange loss is included in *Disbursements* and a foreign exchange gain is included in *Receipts*?

4. Has each transaction been fully and correctly recorded?

If a transaction does not appear on a bank statement, check that the date of the transaction is correct.

5. Have all new accounts which were opened during the accounting period been included?

Dealing with Mutual Funds

When mutual fund companies report distributions, all interest, dividends, gains and losses are reported as a single lump sum. With each distribution, the number of units and the cost per unit change.

If you are separating receipts into *Capital Receipts* and *Revenue Receipts*, the fact that all distributions are reported as a lump sum is problematic for estate accounting purposes. Since gains and losses are 'capital' while interest and dividends are 'revenue', each must be calculated and reported individually as either *Capital Receipts* or *Revenue Receipts*. Re-invested dividends are listed as a purchase in the debit column of the *Investment Account* section.

Investrack

To determine the various amounts, the average cost per unit must be tracked for each mutual fund investment. The last worksheet in the sample spreadsheets is titled *Investrack* and is provided for this purpose. Use individual *Investrack* worksheets to track each mutual fund investment and to make entries for purchases, sales, and distributions. The worksheet formulas will calculate the average cost per unit and gains or losses. A sample *Investrack* worksheet is shown on the next page and includes notes describing the contents of each column.

Investrack Worksheet for Calculating Cost per Unit

1	2	3	4	5	6	7	8
Date of Transaction	Units	Total Units		Total Value	Average Cost per Unit	Amount Paid/Received	Gain or Loss
09-Aug-12	3105.59	3105.590	$25,000.00	$25,000.00	$8.050	$25,000	0.00
20-Sep-12	-123.61	2981.981	-$995.05	$24,004.95	$8.050	$1,000	4.95
23-Sep-12	-618.047	2363.934	-$4,975.28	$19,029.67	$8.050	$5,000	24.72

1 Date that the transaction occurred.
2 The number of units bought or sold as reported in statements from the mutual fund company. A negative number indicates that the units were sold.
3 Running total of units bought or sold; cumulative based on entries in column 2. Used to calculate the average cost per unit.
4 Used to calculate the gain or loss. For purchases, the number in this column is the same as the amount paid as there is no gain or loss on a purchase. For sales, multiply column 2 by column 6 to obtain the total cost for the number of units sold.
5 Running total value of units owned; cumulative based on entries in column 4. Used to calculate average cost per unit.
6 Average cost per unit; column 5 divided by column 3.
7 Actual amount paid or received when mutual funds were bought or sold.
8 To calculate the gain or loss on a sale, subtract column 4 from column 7. A negative number indicates a loss.

29

3. Calculating Compensation

When Compensation Can Be Paid

As an executor or a trustee you can reimburse yourself on a regular basis for legitimate and reasonable expenses which you have paid out of your pocket, such as postage, photocopying, courier, mileage, etc. However, you may not take compensation (payment for the work that you are doing as an executor or trustee) until you have prepared your accounting report, calculated the appropriate compensation amount, and, in some cases, obtained the appropriate approvals.

If the will in which you are named as executor specifies that you may 'pre-take' compensation, you may be paid for the work that you have done before the beneficiaries or the court have approved your accounting. Being pre-paid does not mean that you can be paid before doing some or all of the work expected of an executor. Similarly, a trustee can 'pre-take' compensation if allowed by the terms of the trust.

Pre-taking does not apply to an attorney for property who can be paid on a periodic basis as defined in the *Substitute Decisions Act*. Attorneys may be paid on a monthly, quarterly, or annual basis.

For an estate or a trust, a majority of the capable, adult beneficiaries must approve the accounting. As mentioned in *Chapter 1* (see *Young Beneficiaries or Minors* and *Incapable*

Beneficiaries or Incapable Grantors), the OCL or the PGT or both may need to be provided with the accounting report and a court must approve the accounting if there is a minor or an incapable beneficiary.

If you are named as an executor in a will or as a trustee in a trust document, review the document carefully for any clauses that may affect whether or not you can take compensation or that provide details as to how compensation is to be calculated. Unless a will says something different, if you are receiving a specific monetary gift it is considered a cash gift in lieu of executor's compensation. In other words, you do not get both a cash gift (as opposed to a share of the residue) and executor's compensation unless the will specifically allows you to have both or the beneficiaries agree to your having both. However, as stated earlier, you can be reimbursed for out-of-pocket expenses such as photocopies, couriers, and so on.

One final note about compensation – if an executor, trustee, or attorney takes compensation, it is considered taxable income to that person and must be reported accordingly. If a trust company or a lawyer acts as an executor, trustee, or attorney, compensation may also be subject to sales tax.

Compensation for an Executor or a Trustee

There is no legislation setting out the rates for an executor or a trustee. However, based on numerous court decisions the generally accepted rates are:

- 2 1/2% of receipts,
- 2 1/2% of disbursements,

CALCULATING COMPENSATION

- 2/5 of 1% of the average annual value of the assets as a care and management fee.

For executors, a care and management fee is generally not allowed for the first year of estate administration.

Unless the will specifies otherwise, executors are generally entitled to compensation at the rates listed above. These are slightly less than what is allowed for an attorney for property. A trustee's rate of compensation may be set out in the trust document. If it is not, a trustee can usually anticipate compensation at the same rate as an executor.

Compensation for an Attorney

Unless the Power of Attorney document specifies otherwise, the compensation calculation for an attorney is based on a formula set out in the regulations under the *Substitute Decisions Act* as follows:

- 3% of receipts,
- 3% of disbursements,
- 3/5 of 1% of the average annual value of the assets as a care and management fee.

Factors Considered by a Judge When Reviewing Compensation

If you pass your accounts and a judge reviews your accounting report, she or he will usually consider a number of factors which can be hard to define such as what is a 'fair and reasonable' allowance for your 'care, pains and trouble'. In addition to case law and legislation, most judges will consider the following five factors when determining if the requested compensation is reasonable:

- the magnitude of the trust or estate;
- the care and responsibility involved;
- the time occupied in performing the duties;
- the skill and ability displayed; and
- the success which has attended its administration.

If the assets or transactions are very simple, compensation may be reduced from the usual percentages. On the other hand, if the assets or transactions are numerous or complex, additional compensation may be awarded. Typically, this only occurs if the executor, trustee, or attorney for property has asked for increased compensation. However, increased compensation is not automatically given. It can be difficult to convince a judge to award more than the generally-accepted amounts.

Note that one of the factors a judge may consider is the time spent in performing the duties of an executor, trustee, or an attorney. For this reason, it is important to keep a detailed journal of all activities and time spent acting as an executor, trustee, or attorney. You may be called upon to justify the amount of compensation requested, particularly if you are asking for more than the usual percentages. Keeping a detailed, comprehensive journal is essential if you hope to be successful in claiming compensation beyond the generally-accepted amounts.

Compensation Calculations in the Spreadsheets

The formulas built into the spreadsheets should automatically fill in the total receipts and total disbursements on the compensation worksheet. Before calculating the amount of compensation due, any non-compensable items such as losses on investments, compensation payments, and refunds received must be deducted. By 'non-compensable', we mean items for which you are not allowed to take a percentage as compensation. Any amounts paid directly to you for any reason are generally considered non-compensable. There are other exceptions as well.

As noted above, the formula for calculating a care and management fee varies depending upon whether you are acting as an executor, a trustee, or an attorney. Generally, the calculation of the care and management fee works like this:

1. Determine the average value of assets during the year by adding the assets at the beginning of the year and the assets at the end of the year. Then divide the total by two to obtain the average annual value during the year.

2. Multiply the average annual value by either 2/5 of 1% for an executor or trustee or by 3/5 of 1% for an attorney. If the period of time is less than a full year, it must be pro-rated according to the number of days in the year for which the care and management fee is claimed.

If the formulas in the sample compensation worksheets are not changed, the percentage of compensation on receipts and disbursements should be automatically added to the care and management fee to determine total compensation. Check carefully to ensure that the calculations are done correctly and that any non-compensable amounts have been properly deducted.

Pre-paid Funeral Expenses, Out of Pocket Expenses

If the deceased (or someone on his or her behalf) pre-paid funeral expenses, the pre-paid amount is non-compensable.

Any payments to reimburse an executor, trustee, or attorney for out-of-pocket expenses or for compensation are non-compensable.

Compensation on Tax Refunds

When reporting a tax refund, it is included in *Receipts*. When calculating compensation, tax refunds are non-compensable if the executor, trustee, or attorney overpaid the tax. This can occur inadvertently when, for example, payments are made according to the quarterly tax installment amounts set out in the schedule provided by Canada Revenue Agency (CRA).

There are some circumstances where a tax refund may be a compensable item. However, a full discussion of this topic is beyond the scope of this guide.

Conclusion

If after reading this guide you have any questions, consider meeting with a professional who is familiar with estate accounting and who can provide answers to ensure you get off to a good start.

Glossary

Attorney for Property – a person or trust company named in a valid Power of Attorney for Property signed by a mentally capable person who is 18 or older and properly witnessed. Also referred to as a *substitute decision-maker*. Although the word 'attorney' is used in the USA to mean a lawyer, in Ontario the word does not mean a lawyer; however, a lawyer could be named to act as an attorney for property.

Capital – in estate accounting, the assets that an estate or trust starts with plus any increase in value of those assets that is not treated as *income*.

Continuing Power of Attorney for Property – a *Power of Attorney for Property* is a signed document naming someone to take care of or manage the assets and financial affairs of a person or *grantor*. If the document states that the *attorney's* authority is to continue during the mental incapacity of the grantor, it is referred to as a <u>Continuing</u> Power of Attorney for Property meaning that the attorney can <u>continue</u> to manage the grantor's financial affairs even if the grantor is declared mentally incapable.

Compensation – payment for work done by an executor, trustee, or attorney.

CPP – Canada Pension Plan.

CRA – Canada Revenue Agency, Canada's federal taxing authority.

Disbursement – a payment from an estate, a trust or the grantor's funds; for example, paying a bill, distributing a share of the estate or trust to a beneficiary.

Estate – all of the assets and liabilities of a deceased person or of a living person.

Estate Trustee – another term (used mainly in Ontario) for an executor. An executor is generally named in a will while an Estate Trustee could be named in a will or appointed by the court as an *Estate Trustee with a Will* or an *Estate Trustee without a Will*.

Executor – a person or trust company named in a will to carry out the administration of an estate.

Grantor – the person who 'grants' authority (by signing a Power of Attorney for Property) to an attorney or substitute decision-maker to take care of the financial affairs of the grantor.

Guardian of Property – a person or trust company appointed by court order (usually as a result of a guardianship application being made to the court) to take care of the financial affairs of an incapable person.

Income – in estate accounting, income is what the estate or trust earns or what the grantor receives such as pension income; also referred to as revenue.

Investrack – a worksheet in the spreadsheets provided with this guide that is used to track the value of an investment, particularly mutual funds; the Investrack worksheet is not included in the final accounting report.

Minor – a person under the age of 18 (under Ontario law).

GLOSSARY

Office of the Children's Lawyer (OCL) – an Ontario government authority that must be notified when a person under the age of 18 is a beneficiary, or a potential beneficiary, of an estate or trust.

Passing of Accounts – the court process of having the accounts of an executor, trustee, or attorney for property reviewed and approved by a judge.

PGT – Public Guardian and Trustee, an Ontario government authority with a mandate to deliver services that safeguard the legal, personal and financial interests of certain private individuals and estates.

POA – Power of Attorney.

Power of Attorney for Property – a document signed by a person who is mentally capable and 18 or older in which the person names someone to take care of or manage the assets and financial affairs of that person.

Probate – the process of submitting an application to court to confirm the appointment of an *Estate Trustee with a Will*; also used to refer to a court-appointed *Estate Trustee without a Will* even though 'probate' properly means there is a will to be probated.

Receipt – in estate accounting, a 'receipt' usually means money and other items received on behalf of the estate, trust, or the grantor; it can also mean the paper or electronic proof of a purchase.

Revenue – see *Income*.

Start Date – for an *executor*, the start date is the date of death of the person whose estate is being managed; for a *trustee*, the start date may be the date of death of the person whose will included a trust, otherwise it is the date specified in the trust document; for an *attorney for property*, the start date is the date when the attorney took charge of the grantor's financial affairs; for a *guardian of property*, the start date is as specified in the guardianship order; if an accounting has previously been submitted, the start date is the first day following the end of the previous reporting period.

Substitute Decision-Maker – another name for either an attorney for property or an attorney for personal care; someone who makes decisions for another.

Trustee – a person (or a trust company) who holds and manages assets for someone else; the trustee does not 'own' the assets but is responsible for the care and management of the trust assets as instructed by the terms of the trust document and any applicable laws.

Will – a document, signed by a person who is mentally capable and 18 or older, directing what to do with the person's assets after his or her death and appointing a person ('executor') to carry out those directions.

Acknowledgements

Like many an endeavour, both great and small, this guide would not have been possible without the unwavering support and assistance of family, friends, and colleagues. I gratefully acknowledge their contributions and am especially grateful for their belief in the importance and need for a guide such as this.

First and foremost, thanks to my many clients whose struggles and frustration provided the impetus and who encouraged me to take on this project and see it through to fruition. I dedicate this guide to you and hope that the onerous job of acting as an executor, trustee, or attorney may be eased for you and for others who use this guide.

A huge thanks to my amazing office team who get as excited as I do about projects like this. Finding time (and peace and quiet!) to work on this guide would have been much more challenging if it weren't for my team's continued support. An extra thanks to Lynn Stuckless, Natalie Sanna, and Lisa Meabry for proofreading and offering suggestions along the way.

I gratefully acknowledge the input of my reviewers, Vipin Aggarwal, Nancy Brookes, Glenn Davis, Paul Delfino, Dianne Dodd, Linda Stilborne, and Richard Yasinski. With your different perspectives, you each offered valuable suggestions that helped improve this guide and made it more readable. I appreciate that you gave so generously of your time to read and comment upon the guide.

SIMPLIFIED ESTATE ACCOUNTING

A sincere thank you to Jose Ramirez and Barbara Rainess of Pedernales Publishing LLC. You clearly have a passion for the supportive, wonderful work that you do in bringing an author's manuscript to life in a ready-to-print or ready-to-epublish format so that the work can be shared with others. I am so grateful that I found you.

A heartfelt thank you to my family – my husband, Wayne Wink, steadfast supporter of all my endeavours and proofreader extraordinaire; my daughter, Lorelei Miller, for doing such an outstanding job on the website for this guide and other publications (check out her work at www.eNeffEnterprises.com); and my son, Chris Miller, who ensures my research and writing tools are ready and running smoothly for whenever I am inspired to put pen to paper (or fingers to keyboard).

Lastly, I would like to express my gratitude for Daisy, our yellow lab whose gentle, affectionate presence provided company during those late nights at the office when there was just one more edit to do.

About the Author

Donna is a lawyer with a thriving estates and trusts practice in Ottawa, Ontario, Canada. Her firm, Neff Law Office Professional Corporation, offers services in the areas of wills and trusts, estate planning and administration, powers of attorney, guardianship matters, and real estate sales (www.nefflawoffice.com). Her calm, gentle demeanour and caring spirit are a perfect fit for her areas of practice. As she has experienced such needs within her own family, Donna has a particular interest in estate planning and administration where an individual with a disability is affected.

Donna truly applies a client-centred approach in her practice of law. Always looking for ways to help her clients, her impetus (and inspiration) to write this guide came from the increasing number of clients who struggled with, and who were often intimidated by, the record-keeping duties that their jobs as executors, trustees, and attorneys entailed. Recognizing a lack of available resources and drawing upon her years of experience, she set out to produce an understandable, easy-to-follow guide to fill that void. She is currently writing another book intended for families facing issues related to aging and incapacity and plans to publish it within the next year.

Successful careers as a teacher, a consultant and project manager in the high tech industry, and as a lawyer running her own law practice have provided extensive experience in the development and use of technology in a business setting. Her team can attest to her passion for the latest developments in legal technology and practice management. In 2006, Donna's office took the plunge to paperless and has never looked back. As a result of her enthusiasm and ability to inspire others, she is often called upon to write and speak about her paperless experience as well as practice management and legal technology and estates and trusts issues.

Donna is a member of the Society of Trust and Estate Practitioners, Law Society of Upper Canada, Ontario Bar Association, Canadian Bar Association, and the American Bar Association's Practice Management Section. In April 2010, Donna was appointed to the Planning Board of the ABA TECHSHOW held annually in Chicago. She is past Co-Chair with Dan Pinnington of the Solo and Small Firm Conference and Expo held annually in Toronto. Donna has also been active in her community serving on various boards of local organizations and frequently presenting seminars and workshops to various community groups.

Donna is happily married and a doting grandmother of one. She enjoys all manner of outdoor activities, especially canoeing, geocaching, hiking, cottaging, and enjoys travelling almost anywhere. Donna and her husband live with their yellow lab, Daisy, and a contented old farm cat in an 1870's stone house in a rural area of Ottawa.

www.ingramcontent.com/pod-product-compliance
Lightning Source LLC
Chambersburg PA
CBHW030123170426
43198CB00009B/726